Presented to

Jonah Peake

With love from

The Lighthouse

Date

_9/18/16_

"In the spirit of celebrating children all over the world, the artists in this book have been invited to draw on their own unique and rich cultural heritage in illustrating these biblical stories. Their art is truly a marvelous reflection of how we are all made in God's image."

—Desmond Tutu

Children of God
Storybook Bible

Retold by

DESMOND TUTU

Edited by

Douglas C. Abrams

ZONDERVAN.com/
AUTHORTRACKER
follow your favorite authors

ZONDERKIDZ

Children of God Storybook Bible
Copyright text © 2010 by Desmond M. Tutu
Copyright illustrations © 2010 by Lux Verbi.BM (Pty) Ltd.

Requests for information should be addressed to:

Zondervan, *Grand Rapids, Michigan 49530*

Library of Congress Cataloging-in-Publication Data

Tutu, Desmond.
    Children of God storybook Bible / retold by Desmond Tutu.
        p.   cm.
    ISBN 978-0-310-71912-0 (hardcover)
    1. Bible stories, English.   I. Title.
    BS551.3.T88   2010
    220.9'505—dc22   2009041259

Editor: Barbara Herndon
Art direction & design: Kris Nelson
Cover illustration: Laure Fournier

Printed in China

16 17 18 /LPC/ 23 22 21 20 19 18 17 16 15 14 13 12 11 10 9 8 7

Dear Child of God,

Do you know that God loves you?

The Bible says that each and every one of us – every girl and every boy – is a very special person. God says, "Before you were born, I knew you." God made you just as you are, so you could be your own unique and precious gift to the world.

God made every one of us different – but he loves all of us equally, for we are all God's children. And no matter what happens, God will never stop loving you.

God also wants us to fill our lives with love. Jesus says we should love God, love other people, and love ourselves. How do we do this?

By doing three important things:
    Do what is RIGHT,
                be KIND TO ONE ANOTHER,
                            and be FRIENDS WITH GOD.

You will see these teachings and many more in God's stories, which we have gathered here for you and all of God's children. These stories have been illustrated by some of the most gifted artists I have ever seen. This is truly a storybook Bible created by people in many, many lands for children all around the world just like you.

I hope you enjoy it.

God bless you,

Desmond Tutu

Desmond Tutu

Contents

The Creation

Genesis 1

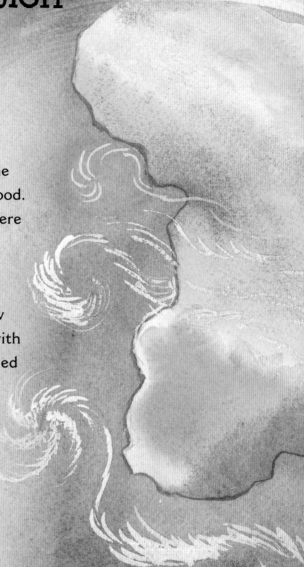

In the very beginning, God's love bubbled over when there was nothing else—no trees, no birds, no animals, no sky, no sea—only darkness.

Out of this love, God spoke. "Let there be light." And there was day. And there was night. And when the first day was done, God smiled and knew that it was good.

On the second day, God said, "Let there be sky where the clouds can float and the wind can blow."

And the sky was bright blue and beautiful.

On the third day, God said, "Let the waters gather together into oceans and let the dry land appear." Now God decided to make the world even more dazzling, with tall trees and long grass. And then the first flower opened in all its glory.

On the fourth day, God said, "Let the sky be filled with the sun and the moon." And God scattered stars across the sky like sparkling diamonds.

On the fifth day…

…God said, "Let there be birds to fly and sing and fish to swim and splash." And the world was filled with the joyous sound of birdsong.

On the sixth day, God said, "Let there be animals—elephants and giraffes, cats and mice, and bees and bugs." And suddenly the world was a very noisy place.

But something was still missing. Then God said, "I will make people, and I'll make them like me so they can enjoy the earth and take care of it." He did just as he had said, and it was all so very, very good.

God looked at everything that he had made and clapped his hands together in delight. "Isn't it wonderful!"

And on the seventh day, God laughed, and rested, and enjoyed his glorious creation.

Dear God,
help me to enjoy and care for your beautiful earth.

God made us to love each other

Adam and Eve

Genesis 2

God breathed the breath of life into the first person and called him Adam.
He put Adam in a beautiful garden called Eden, where there was every kind of delicious fruit to eat. Adam could play all day long and eat whenever he was hungry.

But Adam was lonely.

God said, "My child, it is not good to be alone."

So God brought all the birds and animals to keep him company, but Adam said, "I need a proper friend."

"Yes, you are quite right," God said, and put Adam into a deep sleep. When he awoke, Adam saw that God had made a woman.

"Wow!" Adam said, his jaw dropping in amazement. He had never seen anything so beautiful and so wonderful.

Her name was Eve, and she would be the mother of all people.

Adam and Eve laughed together and loved each other and were happy in the Garden of Eden. God smiled when he saw their joy. He told them to have children so that love and happiness could spread over the whole earth.

Dear God,
thank you for giving us each other to love.

God loves us even when we do wrong

Leaving the Garden

Genesis 3

In the middle of the Garden of Eden grew a very special tree. God said to Adam, "You must not eat the fruit from this tree."

In the garden lived a serpent that liked to make mischief. The serpent said to Eve, "If you eat the fruit from this tree, you will become like God. You will know everything."

The fruit looked ripe and juicy, so Eve picked one and tasted it. Then she handed it to Adam, and he ate too. As they chewed, the fruit began to taste bitter and their smiles turned to frowns.

That evening God walked in the garden and called to them, "Adam! Eve! Where are you?" But Adam and Eve were hiding. They were afraid because they had disobeyed God.

"Why are you hiding from me?" God said. "Did you eat from the tree in the middle of the garden?"

"Eve made me do it," said Adam.

"The serpent made me do it," said Eve.

God let out a deep, disappointed sigh like the wind in the trees at night. Not only had they disobeyed him, they did not even say they were sorry. God punished the serpent, and Adam and Eve had to leave his glorious garden. From then on they had to work hard in the fields to grow food, but God still loved them and watched over them wherever they went.

Dear God,
help me to do what is right and
to remember you love me even when I do wrong.

Noah's Ark

Genesis 6-9

Before long, people started fighting and hurting one another terribly. God wept that they were not enjoying the lovely earth he had made. Finally, he said, "I must make a new beginning. I will send a flood to cover the whole earth."

But one man named Noah was kind and did what was right.

God told Noah to build a big boat called an ark. Then God said, "Gather all your family and two of every kind of animal, bird, and insect." God sent the rain, and Noah led everyone into the ark. For forty days and forty nights it rained so hard that the water covered even the highest mountains.

Boy, did it smell inside the ark! And the noise! The *ROARing* and the *BAAing,* the *NEIGHing* and the *MOOing!* But—amazingly—everyone got along. Yes, even the lion lay down with the lamb.

At last the rain stopped. Noah sent out a dove in search of land. When the bird returned with an olive leaf, Noah and his family cheered. Noah thanked God for saving them.

God told Noah, "I promise not to send another flood to cover the whole earth." And God made a beautiful rainbow so people would never forget his promise.

Dear God,
thank you for rainbows and for keeping your promise to us.

Abraham Trusts God

Genesis 15, 17

Abraham was sad because he and his wife, Sarah, had no children. God told him to pack up everything and to go to a whole new land to begin a whole new life. Abraham trusted God, so he and Sarah left their home and family and began a long, hard journey.

They wandered through deserts, up and down mountains, through green pastures and dark forests, constantly longing for a home of their own filled with happy children. They wandered for so many years they grew too old to have babies. One night, God said, "I am giving this land to you and your children and your children's children."

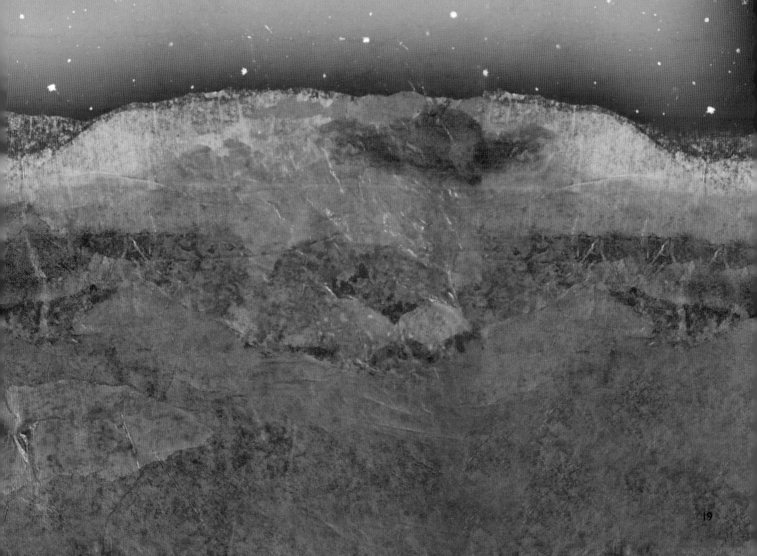

"God, you must be joking! Sarah and I are too old to have children!" Abraham said, stroking his long white beard.

"Trust me, my child," God replied, "look at the stars in the sky. Your children and your children's children will be as many as those stars."

Abraham thought, *How can that be?* But then he remembered that God always keeps his promises. And so Abraham trusted God.

Then God smiled and said, "I will bless you and your children so you can be a blessing to all the people of the world."

Dear God,
help me to be a blessing to others.

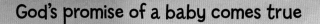

God's promise of a baby comes true

Strange Visitors

Genesis 18

One long, hot day, Abraham was sitting at the entrance to his tent. Three strangers appeared, and Abraham ran to greet them. "Please come and rest," he said. "Here is cool water to wash your feet. I will bring food so you can eat."

Sarah baked bread with her best flour, and Abraham prepared a young calf for a feast. When the food was ready, he served the strangers himself.

The visitors were pleased with how kind and generous Abraham was.

"We are angels sent by God," the visitors said. "When we return, Sarah will have a son."

Sarah was listening from the tent and chuckled. "I am too old to have a baby." The angel said, "Nothing is too hard or too wonderful for God."

And, just as promised, Sarah gave birth to a baby boy. She said, "God has given me a child to bring laughter into my heart."

Abraham and Sarah thanked God and named their son Isaac, which means "laughter."

Dear God,
help me to trust your promises.

A Wonderful Dream

Genesis 25, 27-28

Isaac grew up healthy and strong and had two sons, Esau and Jacob. One day, the brothers fought, and Jacob became scared of his big brother. He ran into the desert to hide. When it was dark, Jacob rested his head on a large, smooth stone and tried to sleep.

For a long time Jacob stared up at the distant stars. Jacob felt far away from his family and so very alone. Finally, he fell into a restless sleep.

He dreamed of a ladder reaching to the sky with angels going up and down. In the dream, God stood beside him and said, "I made a promise to your forefathers, Abraham and Isaac, and I will keep that promise to you. I will be with you, and I will protect you, and I will keep you safe."

Jacob woke up. He was amazed by the dream. "God is in this place, and I did not know it!"

So he took the stone he had rested on, stood it up, and poured oil on it to bless it. He said, "This is the house of God and the gate to heaven." He called that place Bethel, which means "house of God," and he promised to remember God everywhere he went.

Dear God,
help me to see that the whole world is your home.

Joseph Is Sold into Slavery

Genesis 37

Daddy's favorite!" Joseph's brothers sneered.

Jacob had twelve sons, but Joseph really was his favorite. Jacob even made him a special coat of many colors, which Joseph liked to show off.

Joseph told his brothers, "Last night I dreamed that you would all bow down to me." That's when his brothers' jealousy turned to hatred.

One day Jacob sent Joseph to check on his brothers, who were tending the sheep and goats.

When they saw him coming, they said to each other, "Let us kill this dreamer."

Reuben, the eldest, said, "No, he is our brother."

But the others grabbed him, ripped off his coat, dipped it in blood, and took it to their father, Jacob. "A wild animal killed your son," they told him. Jacob was heartbroken and tore his clothes and cried for many days.

But they hadn't really killed Joseph. They had sold him to strangers who took him to be a slave in a faraway land called Egypt. Joseph was scared and did not understand why this was happening, but God was with Joseph and had a special plan for his life.

Dear God,
help me love my brothers and sisters.

Joseph Feeds and Forgives

Genesis 41, 45

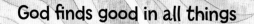

Joseph trembled in front of Pharaoh, the king of Egypt.

"Last night I had a strange dream," Pharaoh said. "I summoned you because I hear you understand the language of dreams."

"It is not I but God who will reveal the meaning of your dream," Joseph said.

"Seven fat cows came out of the river, followed by seven thin cows," Pharaoh said. "And then the thin ones ate up the fat ones!"

"For seven years there will be plenty," Joseph explained, "and then for seven years not a drop of rain will fall, and there will be no food to eat. If you store grain now, there will be enough when the drought comes."

Pharaoh saw that Joseph was wise and made him governor of Egypt. After seven years, just as Joseph had said, there came a terrible drought.

Joseph's brothers came to beg for food and bowed down before the mighty governor. When they realized it was Joseph, they trembled, afraid that he would punish them. But Joseph's love for his family was stronger than his anger. Joseph threw his arms around his brothers and kissed them.

He said, "What you intended for harm, God intended for good. God has used us to save the world from hunger. Bring our family to live in Egypt so they will be safe."

Dear God,
let my love be stronger than my anger.

Moses Is Saved

Exodus 2

Miriam watched her mother place her baby brother into a basket floating on the river. Miriam looked around nervously for soldiers.

It had been many years since Joseph and his brothers had died. Now a wicked Pharaoh ruled Egypt. He had forced Joseph's descendents, called the Hebrews, into slavery and ordered every Hebrew baby boy to be killed.

Miriam's mother cried as she pushed the basket into the reeds. "Watch over him," she said. Miriam quietly followed the basket as it floated down the river.

Her baby brother began to cry. Miriam gasped as she saw one of Pharaoh's daughters coming to bathe in the river. Would she turn the baby over to the soldiers?

Pharaoh's daughter picked the baby up and rocked him gently in her arms. "Poor little thing. This must be one of the Hebrew babies," she whispered. "He needs a mother."

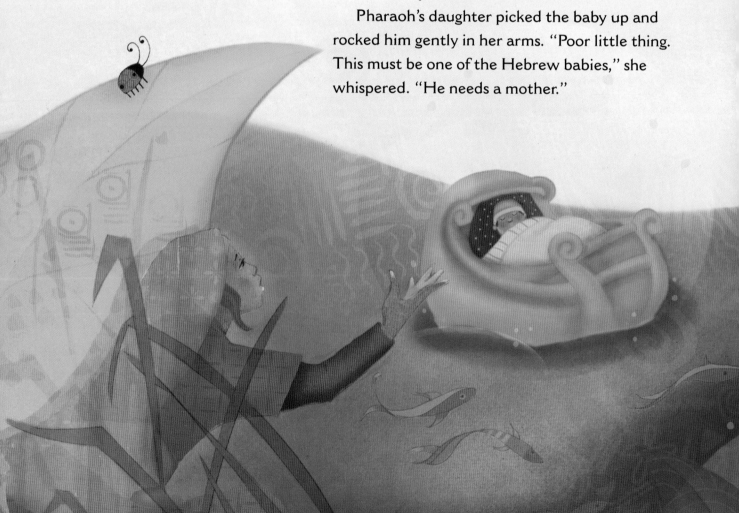

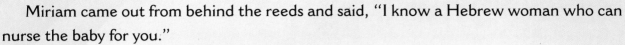

Miriam came out from behind the reeds and said, "I know a Hebrew woman who can nurse the baby for you."

Pharaoh's daughter gave the baby back to his own mother and said, "When he is old enough, bring him to the palace so I can raise him as a prince. I will name him Moses, since I 'drew him out of the water.'"

Dear God,
thank you for loving and protecting your children.

The Voice from the Burning Bush

Exodus 3-4

When Moses grew into a man, he looked after his father-in-law's sheep and goats in the desert. One day he saw a bush burning, but—to his amazement—the leaves were still green! His heart was pounding as he walked closer.

"Moses! Moses!" God called out from the bush.

Moses shook and covered his face with his hands. "Here I am," he said.

"Take off your sandals. You are on holy ground."

Moses did as he was told.

"I am the God of your ancestors. I promised Abraham that I would watch over his family and give them a land flowing with milk and honey. I have heard the cries of the Hebrew people. Go to Pharaoh and tell him to let my people go!"

"Who am I that anyone would listen to me?" Moses asked.

"Moses, I need you to be my lips, my ears, my eyes, my hands so that I may free my children."

"Who will I say has sent me?"

"Tell them I AM WHO I AM sent you."

Moses still trembled, so God said, "Do not be afraid, my child. I will be with you."

Dear God,
let me have the courage to do what you ask of me.

God is with us

Let My People Go

Exodus 7-15

Moses told Pharaoh, "Let my people go." But Pharaoh said, "No!"

So God sent plagues to convince Pharaoh to let the Hebrew people go. First he turned the water into blood. Then he sent frogs and gnats and flies. Then the cattle died, and people and their animals got sores on their skin. There was thunder and hail, and a great cloud of locusts filled the sky. And darkness covered the land for three days. After each plague, Pharaoh agreed to let the Hebrew people go, but then he would harden his heart and say, "No!"

Finally, God wept because now he had to send the most terrible plague of all.

"Mark your doors with lamb's blood," God told Moses to tell the Hebrew families.

On that dreadful night, death passed through the streets, and in every Egyptian family, the firstborn died. The Hebrews called that night Passover because death passed over the Hebrew homes that were marked with lamb's blood and spared their children's lives.

"Go. Be gone!" Pharaoh cried as he held the body of his eldest son. The Hebrews quickly left. But when Pharaoh saw that there was no one to build his pyramids…

33

…he hardened his heart once again. He sent his army to chase the Hebrews down and bring them back into slavery.

The Hebrews fled from Egypt and at last arrived at the edge of the sea. They looked behind them and saw Pharaoh's horses and chariots racing toward them. They were trapped! "God help us!" they cried.

Moses said, "Don't be afraid. God is with us."

God told Moses to hold his staff over the sea. God blew back the water with a mighty wind, leaving a dry path through the sea. The Hebrews crossed over on dry land—the waters forming a wall on their left and on their right.

The Egyptian chariots followed, but their wheels got stuck in the mud. The Hebrews watched in awe as the waters returned and swallowed up Pharaoh's army.

At last, they were really free!

Moses led the people in a song of joy. Then his sister, Miriam, shook a tambourine, and the women sang and danced to thank God for saving them.

Dear God,
help me to bring freedom to all of your children.

The Ten Commandments

Exodus 20

Moses led the Hebrews through the desert to Mount Sinai. Fire and smoke erupted from the mountain, and the ground shook when God spoke in the thunder.

"My children, I brought you out of slavery, and now I will teach you how to live in freedom. All people are my children, but I have chosen you to be a blessing to all the people of the world."

Then God taught the Hebrews his rules for loving him and loving each other:

Put God first.

Do not worship other gods.

Respect God's name.

Keep a day to rest and pray.

Listen to your mother and father.

Do not hurt anyone.

Mothers and fathers must love each other.

Do not take anything without asking.

Tell the truth.

Be thankful for what you have.

When the people heard the voice of God, they promised to love him and obey his rules forever. Moses carved two tablets of stone with the commandments that God had given, so the people would not forget them. After the Hebrews had wandered in the desert for many years, God brought them to a land flowing with milk and honey, just as he had promised. It was the land of Israel.

Dear God,
help me to love you and always to do what is right.

God rewards love and devotion

The Story of Ruth

Ruth 1-4

One year, the rains did not come. There was no food or water in the whole land of Israel, so Naomi and her family left their home in Bethlehem and went to live in the land of Moab. While they were there, Naomi's husband died. Eventually, her sons married Moabite women named Orpah and Ruth. After ten years living in Moab, both of her sons died. Naomi was heartbroken.

She said to Orpah and Ruth, "I am returning to my own land and my own people, and each of you should go back to your mother's house."

Orpah kissed Naomi goodbye, but Ruth clung to her. She loved her as much as her own mother.

"Wherever you go, I will go," Ruth said. "Your people will be my people, and your God will be my God. Where you die, I will die." So Ruth and Naomi wiped their tears and together returned to Bethlehem.

But when they arrived, there was no family left to take care of them. A kind man named Boaz let Ruth pick grain from his field, even though she was a foreigner. When Boaz heard how devoted Ruth had been to Naomi, he fell in love with her. Before long, Ruth and Boaz married. They were the ancestors of Jesus, who would also be born in Bethlehem.

Dear God,
let me love all people no matter where they come from.

39

Samuel in the Temple

1 Samuel 3

A young boy named Samuel lived with a priest named Eli, who taught him to love God with all his heart. But Eli's sons were wicked and did not listen to their father or to God. They did not respect what was holy and took what was not theirs.

One night while Samuel was sleeping, he heard a voice calling, "Samuel! Samuel!" He ran to Eli and said, "Here I am."

"I didn't call you," said Eli. "Go back to sleep."

Samuel lay down, but again he heard someone calling him. He ran to Eli, but was told to go back to bed.

"Samuel! Samuel!" the voice called a third time.

This time Eli understood that it was God calling Samuel. "If you hear the voice again, say, 'Speak, your servant is listening.'"

"Samuel! Samuel!" came the voice yet again.

"Speak, Lord, your servant is listening," Samuel replied.

The next day Eli asked Samuel to tell him what God had said. Samuel was afraid to tell him, but Eli insisted. "God is upset that your sons have behaved badly and plans to punish the wicked."

Eli bowed his head and said, "He is the Lord and will do what he knows is right."

Dear God,
let me hear you when you call.

King David Is Anointed

1 Samuel 16

When Samuel grew up, he became Israel's priest. God said to him, "Go to Bethlehem and find a man named Jesse. I have chosen one of his sons to be king."

Jesse brought all of his sons before Samuel—all except one. He told David, the youngest, to stay in the field to watch over the sheep. He knew that David was too little to be chosen.

David's eldest brother stepped forward first. He was tall and handsome.

"Surely this is the one?" Samuel asked God.

"I do not judge like people judge," God said. "I look into the heart, not at the face."

Jesse brought seven sons before Samuel, but none was the one God had chosen.

"Do you have any other sons?" Samuel asked.

"Only the youngest, David," replied Jesse.

"Send for him," Samuel said.

When David came, Samuel saw in his bright eyes that he had a good heart.

"This is the one," God said.

Samuel took olive oil and poured it on David's head as a sign that he would grow up to be king of Israel. From that day, David was filled with the Spirit of God.

Dear God,
help me to have a good and kind heart.

God helps David defeat a giant

David and Goliath

1 Samuel 17

The Israelites were at war with the Philistines, whose leader was a giant named Goliath.

"Send one man to fight me," he roared. "If he loses, the Israelites will be our slaves forever!"

The Israelites were terrified. No one could beat Goliath.

David's father had sent him to take food to his brothers in the army, and when David heard Goliath's challenge, he said, "I will fight him."

Everyone laughed. "You are just a boy," said King Saul, "and he is a great warrior."

"I am only a shepherd," said David, "but whenever a lion took a lamb from my father's flock, I chased it and rescued the lamb from its mouth."

Since no one else was willing to fight, Saul gave David his sword and shield, but they were too heavy for him. So David took just five smooth stones from the river and his trusty slingshot.

"Come here, boy!" Goliath said, as he drew his sword. "I'll slice you in half and leave your body for the vultures."

"You come with a sword," David replied, "but I come with God on my side." David put a stone in his sling, swung it around, and let it fly. The stone struck Goliath on his forehead, and the giant fell down dead. All the other Philistines gasped and ran away. Many years later, when David became king, the people remembered his bravery in fighting the giant.

Dear God,
help me to be brave.

God makes Solomon wise

King Solomon and the Queen of Sheba

1 Kings 3, 10

After David died, his son Solomon became king, although he was still very young. One night, God said to him in a dream, "Ask for whatever you want, and I will give it to you."

"I want to be wise, to know right from wrong, so that I may be a good king."

God said, "Because you did not ask to be rich or powerful, but to care for your people, I will bless you with both great wisdom and great wealth."

Solomon became famous for his wisdom, and people came from all over the world to ask him questions. In a faraway kingdom, the powerful Queen of Sheba heard of Solomon and decided to test him.

She asked him questions that no one in her kingdom could answer. After each question Solomon closed his eyes for a moment and then told her the answer.

The Queen of Sheba was amazed. "What makes you so wise?"

"All wisdom comes from God," Solomon replied.

"Praise God," she said, "for he has given your people a wise and righteous king."

Dear God,
help me to be wise and make good decisions.

Naboth's Vineyard

1 Kings 21

Next to King Ahab's palace lived a man named Naboth, who owned just one small vineyard. "Give me your land, and I will pay you," said the king.

"This land belonged to my father and his father," replied Naboth. "It is against God's will to sell it."

King Ahab was very upset. He lay in bed and sulked. His wife, Jezebel, asked him what was wrong. "I *want* that vineyard," he whined.

"You are the king, aren't you?" said Jezebel. "If you want it, I will get it for you." She wrote letters telling her officials, "Find two liars to accuse Naboth of saying bad things about God and the king." She signed the letters with the king's seal, and the officials did as they were told.

Poor Naboth was taken away and killed.

Then Jezebel said to Ahab, "He is dead. Go and take his vineyard. It is yours."

But the Lord spoke to the prophet Elijah, who found King Ahab in the vineyard. "God says, 'You have murdered Naboth and stolen his vineyard! I watch over the powerless and punish injustice. Beg for forgiveness or I will destroy you.'"

King Ahab was truly sorry for what he had done. He begged for forgiveness, and God showed him mercy.

Dear God,
help me to protect the powerless.

God uses a young woman to save his people

Esther Saves Her People

Esther 1-10

After many years, the land of Israel was conquered and the Jewish people were taken to live in Persia. One of the Jewish girls was named Esther, and as she grew up, the king of Persia chose her to be his wife. But no one knew, not even the king, that she was Jewish, a descendent of the ancient Hebrews.

Haman, one of the king's advisors, did not like the Jews and told the king that they should be killed.

Queen Esther's cousin Mordecai came to the palace to tell her about Haman's plan. "Please beg the king not to kill our people," he pleaded.

Esther paced back and forth, trembling with fear. "Anyone who goes to the king without being called will be killed."

"God has chosen you, Esther. You are our only hope," Mordecai said, and left.

Esther prayed for courage. Then she went to the king and begged, "Please save me and my people."

"Who wants to harm you?"

"Wicked Haman!" she said, pointing at him.

The king was furious and ordered Haman to be killed on the same gallows that Haman had made for the Jews.

Esther's courage to confront the king saved the Jews, who were filled with great joy and celebrated with a feast to thank God for his protection.

Dear God,
help me to protect my community.

Isaiah Becomes God's Messenger

Isaiah 1, 6

One day while Isaiah was praying in the temple, he had a vision of God sitting on a high throne surrounded by angels singing, "Holy, holy, holy! God is all-powerful and holy! The whole earth is filled with his glory."

Isaiah thought about how unholy the people had become and how they had stopped trusting God. He thought about all the ways the rich were mean and cruel to the poor. Then he remembered all the times he had said hurtful things to others.

Suddenly Isaiah was afraid, for he knew he was not worthy to be in God's presence. "I am lost, for my lips are unclean!" he cried.

52

An angel touched a burning coal to Isaiah's lips. "You are forgiven," the angel said.

Then God said, "Whom can I send to be my messenger?"

Isaiah answered, "Here I am, Lord. Send me."

And God said, "Tell my people, 'If you want to speak to me, come, and I will listen. I will wash away your sins and your hearts will be as white as snow. If you want to be my people, you must be holy. How is one holy? By doing good, seeking what is fair, rescuing the oppressed, and caring for the widow and the orphan.'"

Dear God,
help me to be your messenger of hope and love.

Jeremiah the Boy Prophet

Jeremiah 1, 18

One day, God spoke to Jeremiah. "I have chosen you to be my prophet."
Jeremiah was afraid. "I am only a boy," he said. "I won't know what to say."

"I will tell you the words," God said, touching Jeremiah's lips. "Even before you were born, I chose you."

God showed Jeremiah a branch of an almond tree, which is the first tree to bloom in the spring. Jeremiah knew then what God meant—he would make Jeremiah's work blossom like the almond tree!

Then God sent Jeremiah to a potter's house. Jeremiah watched as the potter formed a jar of clay on his wheel. But the jar was lopsided, so the potter took wet clay and reshaped it until at last it was whole and perfect. "My children are like clay in my hands," God said. "If they let me, I will make them whole and perfect."

Jeremiah served the Lord as a prophet for forty years and tried to teach people how to live and be shaped by God's love.

Dear God,
thank you for giving purpose to everyone's life, including mine.

God Saves Daniel

Daniel 6

Daniel lived in exile in the kingdom of Persia, but he loved God and prayed to him three times every day. Daniel's prayers made him wise, so the king trusted him and asked him for his advice. This made Daniel's enemies jealous.

They tricked the king into making a law that forced everyone to pray only to the king—not to God.

That night, while Daniel was praying, his enemies spied on him.

They ran breathlessly to the king. "Daniel prayed to his God and not to you," they said. "Arrest him!"

The king was very sad because he loved Daniel, but the king had to obey his own law. They arrested Daniel and threw him into the den where the lions were kept. The lions paced back and forth, grumbling and growling and very hungry. "May your God save you," the king said, as a tear fell from his eye.

Daniel prayed, and God closed the mouths of the lions. At daybreak, the king hurried to the den. "Daniel! Daniel!" he called. "Are you alive?"

"I am alive. My God has saved me," Daniel replied.

The king was amazed that Daniel's God had kept him safe and commanded everyone in his kingdom to worship God.

Dear God,
be with me when I am in danger.

God loves everyone, even our enemies

Jonah and the Big Fish

Jonah 1-4

"Go to Nineveh," God said to Jonah. "Tell the people there that if they do not stop their cruelty, I will destroy the city."

Jonah hated the people of Nineveh because they were enemies of Israel. He did not want them to be saved, so he jumped aboard a boat sailing for a faraway country. But God sent a storm. Huge waves crashed over the boat, and it was about to sink. Jonah knew it was because he was trying to run from God. He told the others to throw him overboard so the storm would stop.

Down he plunged into the cold, dark water. Jonah was about to drown when God sent a huge fish to swallow him up. From deep inside the fish, Jonah thanked God for saving him.

The fish burped Jonah out onto the beach.

"Go to Nineveh," God said again. This time Jonah went, and the people listened to him. They asked for forgiveness, and God did not destroy them.

Jonah sat under a shady vine and said, "God, the Ninevites are our enemies! How could you save them?"

God replied, "They are your enemies, but they are my children too."

Dear God,
please help me to love my enemies.

An Angel Appears to Mary

Luke 1

Mary was a young girl living in the village of Nazareth. She was engaged to marry Joseph. One day, the angel Gabriel came to her, saying, "Peace be with you, Mary. God has chosen you for something wonderful."

Mary couldn't believe her ears. "Me? God chose me?" Mary trembled with fear. *What could the angel mean?* "There must be some mistake!" she said.

"Don't be frightened," Gabriel said. "You are going to have a baby boy. You'll name him Jesus."

"You must be joking!" Mary cried. "I'm not even married yet."

Gabriel smiled. "Don't worry, Mary. God will send his Holy Spirit to be with you. Your child will be called the Son of God. Everyone will look on him with wonder. He will be king over all the world, forever and ever."

Mary was amazed. She was going to bring God's Son into the world! Then the angel left, and Mary was filled with joy and her heart sang. "God is good! He remembers the poor and the hungry. He has not forgotten Abraham and Sarah and their descendents. And now I will share in his plan. I will be the mother of Jesus."

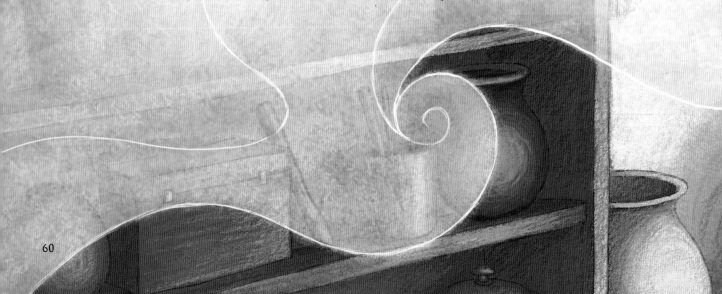

Dear God,
please help me to share in your plan for the world.

Jesus Is Born

Luke 2

The Roman emperor ordered everyone in Judea to go to the town where their father had been born so they could be counted. Mary, by then quite pregnant, traveled to Bethlehem with her husband, Joseph. When they arrived, all the inns were full. Finally, a kind man let them sleep in his stable with the animals.

A cow was *mooing,* and sheep were *baaing.* Then everyone heard the sound of a baby crying. Baby Jesus was born! Mary placed him gently in the manger on a bed of hay. All the animals gathered around and tried to snuffle the new baby with their noses.

Outside the town, shepherds tended their sheep in the fields. Suddenly, the sky lit up and an angel appeared.

"Don't be afraid," said the angel. "I bring the most wonderful news: God's Son has been born in Bethlehem! He will bring great peace and joy to the world. You will find him sleeping in a manger." Soon other angels appeared in the night sky, singing, "Glory to God in the highest!"

The shepherds found Mary, Joseph, and baby Jesus in the stable. They sang songs of praise that filled the night and gave thanks to God for the Savior of the world.

Dear God,
thank you for your Son, Jesus.

The Three Wise Men

Matthew 2

Far across the desert, wise men watched a new star burst into the night sky and knew it was a sign from God that a great king had been born. They followed the star to Jerusalem.

"Where can we find the newborn king?" they asked.

King Herod was shocked to hear about a new king. *Will he take my throne?* he wondered. "Come back to me when you have found the child," he told the wise men.

So they continued on their way, following the star to Bethlehem where they found Jesus in his mother's arms. The wise men bowed down to the baby King and offered him gifts of gold, incense, and myrrh.

But an angel warned the wise men not to tell Herod about the child. So, when they left Bethlehem, they traveled back home by a different road.

When Herod found out that they had left without telling him, he was very angry. "Kill all the baby boys in Bethlehem!" he shouted to his soldiers.

God sent an angel to Joseph in a dream. "Herod is going to look for your baby to kill him," the angel warned. "Take Mary and Jesus across the desert to Egypt. Stay there until I tell you it is safe to come home."

Years later, the angel again came to Joseph in a dream. "Herod is dead," he announced. "It is safe to take Mary and the child home now." The little family packed up and crossed the desert again to find a new home in Nazareth.

Dear God,
protect us when we are in danger.

Jesus Goes to Jerusalem with His Parents

Luke 2

One day, when Jesus was twelve, he traveled with his family to Jerusalem to celebrate the Feast of the Passover. He was so excited that he kept asking his parents, "Are we there yet? I can't wait to see the temple again!"

When the celebration was over, the families from Jesus' village began their journey home. The children were all running and playing together along the way. Mary and Joseph thought Jesus was with his friends. But when they looked for him, he was nowhere to be found. Mary and Joseph were terribly worried!

"We must have left him behind in Jerusalem!" said Mary.

For three days they searched for Jesus in the crowded streets and markets of the city. At last, they went to the temple … and there was Jesus, sitting with the teachers, amazing them with his wisdom and how well he understood God's love.

Mary was very upset. "We have been searching for you everywhere!"

"Why were you searching for me?" Jesus replied gently. "Didn't you know that I would be in my Father's house?"

Jesus had realized that God was his true Father.

Mary's eyes grew wide, and she never forgot that moment. Jesus grew into a man both strong and wise.

Dear God,
help me to speak
with your wisdom.

Jesus Is Baptized

Matthew 3 & Luke 3

Jesus' cousin John wore clothes made from camel's hair. John lived on locusts and wild honey. He was called "the Baptizer" because he was a holy man who called people to the river to wash them clean of their wrongdoing.

"God wants your hearts to be clean as well as your bodies," he told them. "Turn your cruelty into kindness, your selfishness into sharing."

"But how?" the crowd asked.

"If you have two coats, share one. If you have one loaf of bread, share half."

As he took them into the river, John said, "I baptize you with water, but someone far greater than I will come soon. He will baptize you with the fire of the Holy Spirit."

Jesus came to the river and asked to be baptized.

John said, "No, Jesus. *You* should be baptizing *me*!"

Jesus insisted, "This is God's plan."

So John led Jesus into the river and baptized him. As Jesus came out of the water, he saw the heavens open and the Holy Spirit spread its wings over him like a dove.

A voice from heaven said, "This is my beloved Son who fills me with joy."

Dear God,
give me a clean and pure heart.

Jesus in the Desert

Matthew 4

As soon as he was baptized, Jesus went into the desert for forty days to be alone with his Father and pray. He became very hungry and thirsty. The Devil came to tempt Jesus and said, "If you are God's Son, then change these stones into bread."

Then Jesus answered, "Scripture says, 'People can't live on bread alone. God's Word is even more important than food.'"

Then the Devil took him to the very top of the temple in Jerusalem. "If you are God's Son, throw yourself off the building. Doesn't Scripture say, 'God will send angels to catch you'?"

Jesus replied, "Scripture also says, 'You must not test God.'"

Then the Devil took Jesus to the top of a high mountain, looking out over all the kingdoms of the world. "I will give you power over everyone if you will bow down and worship me!" he said.

"Go away, Satan!" Jesus cried. "The earth belongs to God alone, and he is the only One who must be worshiped."

As the Devil disappeared, angels came to comfort Jesus.

Dear God,
help me to trust you when I am tempted.

Jesus Turns Water into Wine

John 2

Jesus and his disciples went to a wedding at Cana in Galilee with his mother, Mary. Everyone was having fun, but Mary noticed that the wine had run out. Afraid the party would be spoiled, she went to Jesus and whispered, "They have no more wine."

"Mother, why are you coming to me?" Jesus replied. "I am not ready yet."

But Jesus *was* ready. Mary knew it in her heart. She told the servants, "Do as he says."

Jesus pointed to six large stone jars. "Please fill them with water." The servants filled them right to the brim.

"Now," said Jesus, "fill a cup and take it to the master of the banquet to taste." So they did.

The man drank some, although he did not know where it had come from. He smacked his lips and called the bridegroom to one side. "This is the best wine I've ever tasted. Where is it from?"

The bridegroom didn't know, but Mary smiled to herself, knowing that everything Jesus gave was holy.

Jesus had turned the water into wine. This was his first miracle.

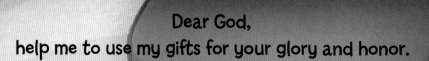

Dear God,
help me to use my gifts for your glory and honor.

Jesus Goes Fishing

Luke 5

One sunny morning, Jesus stood at the edge of Lake Galilee teaching people how they could live with joy in their hearts. As he spoke, more and more people crowded around to hear. Jesus had to step into a boat owned by Simon, the fisherman.

Jesus sat down and from there began teaching the people who had gathered on the shore.

When he finished teaching, Jesus said, "Let's go fishing."

Simon replied, "Master, we've been fishing all night and didn't catch a thing." Then he sighed. "But if you want us to try again, we will."

So they took the boat out into the deep water, and Simon and the other fishermen threw the nets into the sea. Soon they had caught so many fish that the boats almost began to sink.

Amazed, Simon fell to his knees. "Master," he said, "I am not good enough to be near you."

"Don't be afraid," Jesus said. "Follow me and you will not just catch fish, you will catch people for God."

Simon and the other fishermen left their boats on the beach and followed Jesus. They became his first disciples.

Dear God,
help me to follow you.

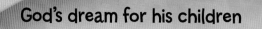

Jesus Teaches the Secret of Happiness

Luke 6

One day, Jesus told his followers about God's dream of a world where all the children of God are loved and cared for, and no one is left out.

Blessed are you who are poor, for all God's world is yours.
Blessed are you who are hungry, for God will feed you.
Blessed are you who are sad, for God will comfort you and you will laugh again.

Blessed are you who feed the poor, for you are the hands of God.
Blessed are you who comfort the sad, for you are the arms of God.
Blessed are you who work for peace, for you are the voice of God.
Blessed are you who are loving and kind, for you are the heart of God.

You are the light of the world. Shine! Let the world see your
goodness and therefore give glory to your Father in heaven.

If you are angry with your brother or sister, speak to them from your heart and
make peace. Forgive and you will be forgiven. Love your enemies and pray for them,
for they, too, are children of God. Do to others as you would have them do to you. What
you give to the world, so the world will give to you.

Dear God,
thank you for showing us the way to true happiness.

Jesus Blesses the Little Children

Mark 10

Jesus spent many hours teaching people about God and how he loves us all. One day, when Jesus was tired and resting, some parents arrived with their children. The children were giggling and laughing and running around making noise while their parents asked the disciples if they could speak with Jesus.

"What do you want with the Master?" asked the disciples.

"We want him to bless our children."

"The Master is resting," the disciples said. "You can't bother him now. Go home." But Jesus heard them. "Do not chase away the children!" he called. "Let them come to me. God loves children, and when they smile, he smiles; when they laugh, he laughs; when they cry, he cries."

Jesus went to the children, and they laughed and played together for a while. He took them in his arms and hugged them. He placed his hands on their heads and blessed them. Then he told the disciples, "Everyone who wants to see God's dream come true must see with the eyes of a child."

Dear God,
help me to see your dream.

The Good Neighbor

Luke 10

Jesus said, "All you need to remember is to love God and love your neighbor as much as you love yourself."

"But who is my neighbor?" a teacher asked.

Jesus told a story to explain.

"One day, a Jewish man was robbed and wounded and left lying in the road.

"A little while later, a priest walked by, but he pretended he didn't see the injured man.

"Soon, another man came by. He worked at the temple, but he didn't stop either.

"At last, a Samaritan came down the road. His people were enemies of the Jews. But the Samaritan stopped! He got off his donkey and gently bandaged the man's wounds. Then he put him on his donkey and walked beside him to the nearest inn. He put him to bed and took care of him.

"Now," asked Jesus, "which of these people was a good neighbor?"

"The Samaritan," replied the teacher.

"That's right," said Jesus. "You are all part of the same family—God's family. God wants you to be like him, loving and kind to everyone—even your enemies."

Dear God,
help me to love my enemies and see them as my family.

God gives us the Great Commandment

The Law of Love

Mark 12

Sometimes it seems like there are so many rules. It is often hard to know which ones are most important. In Jesus' time, people argued about which rule was most important to God.

One of the elders, bent over with age and wisdom, heard Jesus teaching his followers. The elder thought to himself, *Wow! This guy really knows what he is talking about.* The elder leaned on his cane and scratched his white hair. "You seem very wise. Tell me, what is the most important rule of all?"

"There are two," Jesus replied. "The first is to love God with all your heart, with all your soul, with all your mind, and with all your strength. The second is to love everyone as much as you love yourself."

The elder nodded. "You are right," he said. "The greatest gift we can offer God is to love him and love his children."

Dear God,
fill me with love.

The Disciples Learn to Pray

Luke 11

Jesus was praying under a fig tree. When he was done, his disciples said, "Jesus, we want to open our hearts to God like you. Please teach us how to pray."

"Praying is easy," Jesus said. "God wants to know you and bring you close. Just speak to God like a friend and he will listen. God hears your softest whisper, and even when you can't find the words, God hears what's in your heart."

"But how do we begin?" the disciples asked.

"You can start like this," said Jesus.

"Loving Father in heaven, blessed is your name.
May your dream of love and peace come true,
and may the whole world be made new.
Give us each day the food we need to live.
And help us to forgive so we may be forgiven."

Jesus continued, "What do you truly need? Ask and it will be given; search and you will
find; knock and the door will open. Trust God in everything, for you are his children."

Dear God,
help me to open my heart to you.

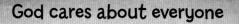

God cares about everyone

The Lost Sheep

Luke 15

All sorts of people flocked to hear Jesus. Some followed God's ways, and some did not. Jesus treated everyone with love and kindness. Some of the teachers did not like this, and they complained. "Just look at him, sitting down and eating with *those* people! I would never!"

Jesus heard their grumbling, so he told them a story.

"Once there was a shepherd who had one hundred sheep, including an old, smelly ram that was always getting into trouble. One day the old ram wandered off. The shepherd could have said, 'Good riddance! That one was nothing but a nuisance.' But he did not. Leaving the other ninety-nine perfectly well-behaved sheep, he searched all night in the cold and rain.

"At last, the shepherd found that old ram in a ditch. He was covered with mud. Boy, did he smell! But the shepherd didn't mind one bit. He put the ram on his shoulders and carried him all the way home singing. Then he called his friends and had a party. 'I have found the sheep that was lost!' he shouted.

"It is the same in heaven," Jesus explained. "The angels have a party every time someone who was lost comes back to God."

Dear God,
help me to care about everyone.

God provides enough for everyone
Jesus Feeds the Crowd

John 6

All day in the hot sun, thousands of people sat and listened to Jesus talk about God's dream. They were so hungry to know God, they forgot to eat lunch!

When the sun started to go down, Philip said, "Master, it's late and the people are hungry. You should send them home."

"Why send them home?" said Jesus. "Just feed them."

"Feed them?!" Philip said. "We don't have any food."

"Someone has something to share," Jesus answered.

A little boy offered to share his five small loaves of bread and two tiny fish. Philip threw his arms in the air. "That's not enough for all of these people!"

"Ask the people to sit down," Jesus said. He took the bread in his hands, looked up to heaven, and blessed it. He did the same with the fish. Then he told the disciples to hand out the food.

They were amazed! There was more than enough for everyone. When all the people had finished eating, the disciples filled twelve baskets with the food that was left!

With God's love, five loaves and two small fish fed more than five thousand people.

Dear God,
help me to share so there will be enough for everyone.

Jesus the Healer

Luke 5

One day, a man rushed up to Jesus and threw himself on the ground. People were pointing and shouting at him to go away, because his skin was covered with big, ugly sores and bumps. They were afraid they would catch his disease if they touched him.

"Lord, if you are willing, please heal me," he pleaded.

Jesus reached out his hand and touched him, "Yes, I am willing."

The man's disease disappeared.

Another time, there was a man who could not walk, so his friends carried him on his bed to Jesus. When they reached the house where Jesus was teaching, there were so many people they could not push through the crowd. The lame man's eyes filled with tears knowing he would never walk again.

"It's okay, just take me home."

"No," one of his friends said. "We won't give up on you."

So his friends climbed up to the roof of the house, took some tiles off, and lowered the bed until their friend lay right in front of Jesus.

Jesus was amazed by the faith of this man and his friends. "You are healed. Get up and walk."

The man stood up, took one step, then another, and danced home praising God.

Dear God,
help me to care for those who are sick.

Jesus Restores Sight and Gives Life

Mark 5, 8

A blind man felt his friends pulling him through the noisy crowd. *Is Jesus really going to be able to heal me?* he wondered. At last he heard one of his friends pleading, "Master, we beg you. Touch our friend so he can see again."

Then the blind man felt Jesus' hands gently touch his eyes.

"Can you see anything?" Jesus asked.

"I can see people, but they look like trees walking around."

So Jesus put his hands onto the man's eyes again. This time the man looked around in wonder, "Wow! Now I can see clearly!"

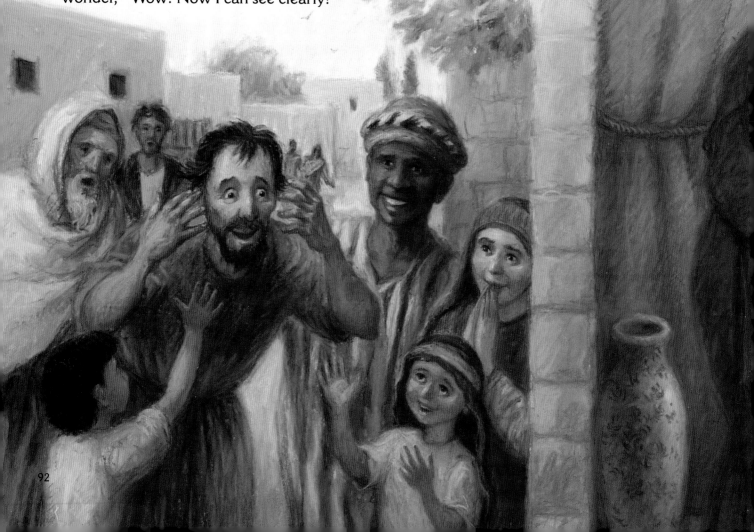

Another time, a man named Jairus ran to Jesus with tears streaming down his face. "Please, Master, my daughter is dying. Come quick."

When they got to Jairus' house, the girl had already died, and everyone was weeping.

"Don't cry," Jesus said. "She's just sleeping."

Jesus took Jairus and the girl's mother into the room where she lay. He took the little girl's hand and said, "Child of God, wake up!" She immediately sat up in bed!

Then her stomach growled. Jesus smiled and said, "Feed her. She's hungry."

Dear God,
thank you for healing me when I am sick.

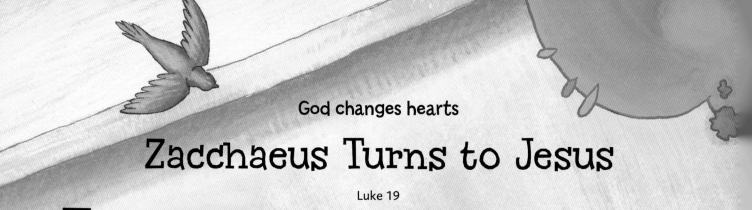

God changes hearts

Zacchaeus Turns to Jesus

Luke 19

Zacchaeus wanted to see Jesus, but he was too short to see over the crowd. He stood on tip-toes and jumped up and down. He tried to squeeze through to the front, but no one would let him.

Why doesn't anybody like me? he wondered. But he knew the reason. Zacchaeus was a tax collector who had become rich by cheating the townspeople.

Then Zacchaeus spied a tree. *Aha!* he thought to himself. *I will climb that tree and have the best view of all.*

Then Jesus stopped under that very tree and looked up at him.

"Zacchaeus," Jesus called out, "climb down, for I am coming to your house today." Zacchaeus could not believe his ears. He jumped down and ran home to get ready.

"That man is a liar and a cheat," the townspeople said. "Why is Jesus going to his house?"

Zacchaeus realized they were right and he was ashamed. When Jesus entered his house he said, "Lord, I will give half of everything I own to the poor, and everyone I have cheated I will pay back four times the amount I stole."

Jesus smiled. "Dear Zacchaeus," he said, "today you have become a new man. Now you can truly stand tall."

Dear God,
help me to be honest and fair.

The Loving Father and the Son Who Came Home

Luke 15

Jesus told a story about God's love and forgiveness.

"A man had two sons. The younger said to his father, 'I don't want to wait until you die. Give me my inheritance now so I can do what I want.' The elder son was shocked, but his father did as he was asked, and the younger son left home.

"He quickly wasted it all, and when the money had run out, no one would give him anything to eat. Eventually he got a job taking care of pigs. He lived with pigs, ate with pigs, slept with pigs, and smelled like a pig! He was so hungry even the slop the pigs ate looked good to him.

"'My father's servants have plenty, and here I am starving!' he said to himself. 'I will go home and beg my father to let me be a servant on his farm.'

"When his father saw his youngest son coming down the road, he ran to meet his son and threw his arms around him and kissed him. 'No, Father,' said the younger son. 'I am not good enough to be your son. Just let me be a servant on your farm.'

"'Quick,' his father said to his servants, 'prepare a feast!'

"When the elder son came home and saw the celebration, he was angry.

"'You throw a feast for that no-good son of yours?' he said to his father.

"'Both of you are my sons,' his father said, 'and I will never stop loving you. One of my boys was lost and now is found.'"

Dear God,
thank you for always forgiving my
mistakes and welcoming me home.

Jesus Calms the Storm

Luke 8 & Matthew 8

Let's go to the other side of the lake," Jesus suggested one day, wanting to find a quiet place to rest. He and his disciples got into a boat and started sailing. Bright sunlight sparkled on the water, and gentle waves rocked Jesus to sleep.

But while he napped, the wind began to blow, and waves crashed onto the deck. The boat was filling with water, and the disciples were terrified it would sink.

"Master, Master!" they cried. "Wake up! We are going to drown!"

Jesus stood and spoke quietly to the wind, "Calm, be gentle." And to the waves he said, "Peace, be still."

Suddenly the wind stopped blowing, the waves stopped crashing, and all was peaceful once again.

Jesus turned to his friends, "Why were you afraid? Don't you trust God to protect you?"

The disciples stared at each other with their mouths hanging open in amazement. "Who is this man?" they whispered. "Even the wind and the waves obey him."

Dear God,
help me to trust you when I am afraid.

Sharing God's Plan

Matthew 25

Jesus said, "In time, God will gather all people together and will separate them like a shepherd separates the sheep from the goats.

"To those who helped God's dream come true, he will say, 'You are blessed, for I was hungry, and you gave me food; I was thirsty, and you gave me water; I was a stranger, and you welcomed me; I was naked, and you gave me clothes; I was sick, and you cared for me; I was in prison, and you visited me.'

"Those who were generous will say, 'But Lord, when were you hungry or thirsty? When were you a stranger or needing clothes? How could you be sick or in prison?'

"God will answer, 'As you did for even the least of my children, you did for me.'

"Those who were not generous will say, 'Hey, wait a minute, God! If we had realized that it was *you*, we would have helped too.'

"God's tears will fall as he says, 'It is too late. Every time you turned away from one of my children, you turned away from me.' "

Dear God,
help me to see you in everyone I meet.

Jesus Is Changed on the Mountaintop

Matthew 17

Jesus said to his closest friends, Peter, James, and John, "Come with me to the mountaintop to pray."

They climbed for hours until their legs ached. At last they were at the top. Jesus' face began shining with a light as bright as the sun, and his clothes seemed to glow. Moses and Elijah, two great leaders who had died long ago, appeared next to Jesus and began to talk with him.

Peter and his friends were stunned. "Lord," Peter gasped, "we are blessed to be here. Let me build houses, and we can stay in this wonderful place forever!"

But even as he was speaking, a bright cloud came down and covered them all. A voice spoke from the cloud.

"This is my Son who fills me with joy. I love him. Listen to what he says."

Peter, James, and John covered their heads and threw themselves on the ground in fear. Jesus touched them gently on the shoulder. The cloud had gone, and Jesus was alone with them.

"We cannot stay on the mountaintop," Jesus said. "We must return to the valley where God's children need us."

Dear God,
help me to share your glory with others.

A Woman's Love for Jesus

John 12

Jesus was at the home of friends who had given a dinner in his honor. He was eating and drinking at the table and having a good time when a woman came in. She had long, black hair and was carrying a jar of precious perfume. She broke the top off the jar, and instantly the house was filled with the loveliest smell of lavender. The woman poured the perfume onto Jesus' feet and wiped them with her hair.

Some of Jesus' disciples were shocked. "What a waste!" they said. "That perfume is very expensive. She should have given it to us to sell so we could give the money to the poor."

"There will be many other times when we can help the poor," Jesus said. "This woman is preparing my body for when I die. She has done something very beautiful— she is showing me how much she loves me. What she has done today will be remembered forever."

Dear God,
let me be generous with my love.

Jesus Becomes a Servant

John 13

Jesus and the disciples gathered in Jerusalem. Their feet were dirty from walking the dusty roads telling people about God's dream. The disciples started arguing over which one of them was the greatest.

Jesus got up and tied a towel around his waist. He took a basin of water and began to wash the feet of his friends and to dry them on the towel.

Jesus' friends were shocked. "That is a servant's job!" they shouted.

But Jesus quietly continued washing their feet. When it was Peter's turn, he jumped up. "Master, you will never wash my feet!"

"Then you cannot be my disciple," said Jesus.

"Lord," cried Peter, "wash my feet, my hands, my head, all of me!"

After Jesus had finished washing their feet, he took off the towel and sat down again.

"Do you understand what I have done?" he asked. "You call me Lord and Teacher, but I have washed your feet like a servant. You must follow my example. The leader is the servant of all. You must be as servants to each other. No one is more important than anyone else. I want you to love one another the way I love you."

Dear God,
help me to be a willing servant of all.

Jesus Shares His Last Meal with His Friends

Matthew 26

Jesus wanted to celebrate Passover and share a meal with his disciples so he could say good-bye. By that time, many people looked up to Jesus as a great leader. This made some of the priests and the Roman rulers very jealous. Jesus knew that they wanted to arrest him and that his life was in danger. Jesus knew it was time for him to return to his Father.

As they all sat around the table, he picked up a loaf of bread. After thanking God, Jesus broke the bread and passed a piece to each of them.

"This bread is my body," he said.

Then he took the cup of wine. Again he thanked God and passed it around to his friends.

"This is my blood," he said. "I am pouring it out for you. Whenever you break bread and drink wine like this, remember me and remember that someday God's dream—of everyone sharing and caring, loving and laughing—will come true."

Dear God,
thank you for making me part of your dream.

The Trial and Death of Jesus

Matthew 26-27

After Jesus' last supper with his disciples, they went out to the Garden of Gethsemane. Jesus stayed awake, praying alone. Suddenly, soldiers surrounded them and arrested Jesus. They accused him of trying to become king.

At his trial the Roman ruler, Pontius Pilate, asked, "Are you the king of the Jews?"

"My kingdom is not of this world," answered Jesus.

"Set him free," said Pilate. "This man has done nothing wrong."

But some people were angry. "He called himself a king," they shouted. "Crucify him!"

To please the crowd, Pilate ordered the soldiers to beat Jesus and then to kill him. They whipped him and made fun of him. Pretending he was a king, they put a crown of thorns on his head and a red cloak around him. Then they made him carry a heavy, wooden cross to a hill outside the city.

They nailed Jesus to the cross. His mother, Mary, and several other women wept at his feet and stayed with him until the very end.

Then Jesus prayed to God one last time before he died. "Father, forgive them, for they do not understand your dream."

Dear God,
help me to forgive just as Jesus forgave.

God raises Jesus from the dead

Jesus Is Alive

Luke 24 & John 20

Two days after Jesus died, Mary and several other women went to the tomb where he had been buried. They were shocked to see that the stone that had covered the opening had been rolled away. They looked inside. Jesus' body was gone! Two angels in dazzling clothes said, "Why are you looking for Jesus here? Jesus is alive! Go tell the others." The women rushed to tell the disciples. At first, no one believed them.

A little while later, the disciples gathered to talk about what had happened. Suddenly, Jesus stood right in front of them.

"Peace be with you," Jesus said.

The disciples were so frightened they clutched each other and trembled. But Jesus said, "Don't be afraid, it is me. Look at my hands and my feet. Touch me." But they still could not believe that Jesus was alive.

"Give me a piece of fish," said Jesus. He took the fish and ate it, and his followers were convinced. Jesus really was alive and back with them again! They were so happy, they laughed and clapped their hands in joy.

Dear God,
help me to see that Jesus lives.

The Good News

Acts 1

Jesus stayed with his friends and spoke to them about all the things that had happened to him. He reminded them of the old stories, about how the prophets had promised that God would send his Son to help God's dream come true.

Jesus said, "Tell everyone everywhere that God loves them, and that those who believe in the good news of God's dream should be baptized. And in a few days you, my friends, will be baptized with the Holy Spirit."

He then stretched out his hands and blessed them, saying, "I will be with you always, to the end of time." A cloud came from heaven, and Jesus disappeared.

The disciples stared up into the sky looking for him.

Two men in white robes appeared. "Why are you looking up into heaven?" they said. "Jesus is not far away. He will always be close to you even though you cannot see him. And one day, he will return in the same way that he left you."

The disciples went home singing praises to God.

Dear God,
help me to know that Jesus is near.

The Coming of the Holy Spirit

Acts 2

The disciples were in Jerusalem. They were all so very excited. They could feel that something wonderful was about to happen.

Early one morning, *whoooosshhhh!* A strong wind blew through the room where they were gathered. The house shook. Lights like tongues of fire rested on everyone's head, and they felt the power of God's Holy Spirit inside them.

Their hearts filled with love, and they began to talk. But they were talking in different languages—Greek and Latin, Egyptian and Libyan, and even Arabic!

At that time, Jerusalem was crowded with visitors from all over the world. When the people heard the noise of the wind, they all hurried to see what had happened. The visitors were amazed to find the disciples speaking so many different languages.

Peter spoke to the crowd. "What was prophesied has come true," he said. "God has made Jesus both our Savior and Friend. Through him, God's wonderful dream is coming true."

"What can we do to realize God's dream?" the people cried.

Peter said, "Return to God and be baptized so your sins will be forgiven. You will be given a new life, and you too will receive the gift of the Holy Spirit."

Three thousand people were baptized that day.

Dear God,
fill me with your spirit.

The Disciples Spread the Good News

Acts 2-4

Every day the disciples went out into the street telling everyone they met that Jesus was alive and that he was bringing God's love and peace to the world. They invited everyone to turn away from doing wrong and become part of God's dream with Jesus.

A crippled beggar outside the temple called out to Peter, "Have pity on me. Give me money so I can eat."

Peter said, "I have no silver or gold, but I will give you what I have. In the name of Jesus, stand up and walk."

Peter touched the beggar, and his legs became strong. He leapt to his feet and jumped for joy, praising God.

More and more people joined the new church. Some people sold their houses and their land. Everyone shared whatever they had with those who had nothing. They were filled with joy and love for one another, and love for God. They became one big, happy family sharing everything together, just like God had always dreamed it could be.

Dear God,
help me to share my love for you.

Paul Follows Jesus

Acts 9

The temple leaders were jealous of all the people following Jesus. They had many put in jail. Some were even killed. The believers were especially afraid of one man. His name was Saul.

One day, Saul was on his way to arrest Jesus' followers in Damascus. Suddenly, he fell to the ground, blinded by a brilliant light.

He heard a voice saying, "Saul, Saul, why are you attacking me?" It was Jesus speaking to him!

For three days, Saul was blind and did not eat or drink. On the fourth day, he had a change of heart. Now he believed that Jesus was the Son of God!

Saul was baptized. He changed his name to Paul. He wrote many letters to encourage the new churches in distant lands.

Many people asked Paul questions, including what was most important to God. Paul answered, "Faith, hope, and love, but the greatest of these is love."

"But what is love?" they asked.

"Love is patient. Love is kind. Love does not envy or boast. It is not arrogant or rude. It does not insist on its own way. It is not irritable or resentful. It rejoices not in wrongdoing, but in truth and justice and forgiveness."

Dear God,
please give me faith, hope, and love.

The Promise of a New Earth

Revelation 21-22

When the disciple John was very old, God sent him dreams and visions. He saw that there would be wars and famines and floods and terrible disasters. But God told John, "Soon I will make a new heaven and a new earth. Then every tear will be wiped away. I will be with my people, and they will be with me. Everyone will live in peace and joy."

God showed John a vision of this holy place. It glittered with gold and precious stones, and the sky was so bright there was no need for the sun or moon to give light.

"From this place," God said, "will flow the river of life, and from it I will give the water of life to everyone who is thirsty. On either side of the river will be the tree of life, and the leaves of the tree are for the healing of the nations. You are my children. You are all brothers and sisters together, my family. Come and drink, my beloved children, from the water that gives you life, love, and joy!"

Dear God,
help me to make your dream of a new earth come true.

Illustrators

Kristin Abbott
United States

The Creation

Laure Fournier
France

Samuel in the Temple
God Saves Daniel
An Angel Appears to Mary
Jesus Blesses the Little Children
Zacchaeus Turns to Jesus

Alik Arzoumanian
United Kingdom/United States

Naboth's Vineyard
The Disciples Learn to Pray
The Coming of the Holy Spirit

Jago
United Kingdom

King David Is Anointed
The Three Wise Men
Jesus Goes Fishing
The Good News

Lyuba Bogan
Russia/United States

The Voice from the Burning Bush
Jesus Restores Sight and Gives Life
The Trial and Death of Jesus

Cathy Ann Johnson
United States

Presentation page
Moses Is Saved
King Solomon and the Queen of
   Sheba
Jesus Teaches the Secret of Happiness
Jesus Becomes a Servant
The Lost Sheep

Paddy Bouma
South Africa

The Ten Commandments
Jesus Is Born

EB Lewis
United States

Jesus Shares His Last Meal
   with His Friends

Shane Evans
United States

Jesus the Healer
Paul Follows Jesus

Frank Morrison
United States

Strange Visitors
A Woman's Love for Jesus

LeUyen Pham
Vietnam/United States

Joseph Is Sold into Slavery
Jesus Goes to Jerusalem
  with His Parents
Jesus Turns Water into Wine

Marjorie Van Heerden
South Africa

A Wonderful Dream
Sharing God's Plan

Jesse Reisch
United States

Noah's Ark

Beatriz Vidal
Argentina

Adam and Eve
The Story of Ruth
Jesus Is Alive
Jesus Calms the Storm

Javaka Steptoe
United States

Abraham Trusts God

Stefano Vitale
Italy

Leaving the Garden
Isaiah Becomes God's Messenger
Jesus in the Desert
The Law of Love
The Promise of a New Earth

Peter Sutton
United Kingdom

Let My People Go
Jesus Feeds the Crowd
Jesus Is Changed on the Mountaintop

Nadine Wickenden
United Kingdom

Joseph Feeds and Forgives
David and Goliath
The Loving Father and the Son Who
  Came Home

Marijke Ten Cate
The Netherlands

Esther Saves Her People
Jonah and the Big Fish
Jesus Is Baptized
The Good Neighbor
The Disciples Spread the Good News

Xiao Xin
China

Jeremiah the Boy Prophet

125

Acknowledgments

Creating a global Children's Bible requires the God-given talents of many people around the world. So many individuals have collaborated and worked tirelessly that I fear I may not do their hard work justice.

I should begin with my friend and fellow Anglican priest, Luke Stubbs, who conceived the idea of this Bible and who worked on it faithfully and zealously, literally until the day he died. It was his conviction that this Bible was needed to help share God's love around the world, and it is to his memory that the book is dedicated. His wife, Helen Brain, shared Luke's belief in this labor of love and helped in the collection and preparation of the Bible stories to be included. We grieve with Helen and her children for their great loss.

We cannot thank Luke's colleagues at Lux Verbi.BM enough for sharing the vision for the project, wholeheartedly supporting Luke and taking over after Luke's illness. Managing director Stephan Spies spared nothing to make the best Children's Bible possible and to share it with publishers around the world. Heartfelt thanks also to the rest of the development team: Willie Botha (publications manager and theological advisor), Eben Pienaar (marketing manager and developer of audio and DVD recordings), Ewald van Rensburg (theological and text advisor), Elzette Hansen (text editor), Anna-Marie Petzer (DTP development), Stefan Dippenaar (production manager), and especially Johan van Lill, the dedicated and brilliant project manager who worked around the clock to bring the stories and the illustrations together. I am also grateful for the unflagging commitment of the Lux Verbi.BM national and international sales teams, under Koos Fouché and Noeline Neumann.

In the United States, our boundless gratitude to Lux Verbi.BM's project partners at Zondervan, who worked closely with them at every step of the project. Thanks especially to Annette Bourland (senior VP & publisher) for casting the vision of this book as being a gift to the world, to Barbara Herndon (acquisitions editor) and Kris Nelson (senior art director) for weaving the text and artwork together so beautifully, and to Alicia Mey (VP of marketing), Helen Schmitt (senior marketing director), and their marketing team for giving the message of this book a platform to speak to children everywhere.

My sincere appreciation to CLF (Christian Literature Fund) South Africa for their financial and editorial support, which made the African vernacular language editions possible: Willem Botha (CLF chairperson), Christelle Vorster (manager), Amanda Carstens (head of publications), and Dr. Gideon van der Watt (editor and project leader – vernacular texts). CLF is one of the most active organizations in supporting the production of Christian material in African vernaculars.

In my office, I want to thank Lavinia Browne, who also shared her literary skills, and Vivian Ford and Tamu Matose for their ongoing assistance to me and to this project.

Lynn Franklin, my agent and beloved family member, worked with unparalleled dedication on every detail of the Bible to ensure its quality and that all the children of the world are reflected in its pages.

Doug Abrams, my creative and skilled friend and editor, worked closely with me to make sure that the stories remained true to Scripture and to my understanding of God's love. Doug was aided greatly by Reverend Steven DeFields Gambrel. They each have a gifted writer's sensitivity to language and a father's knowledge of a child's heart. This Bible would not have been the work it is without their help and guidance.

I also want to thank the incredibly gifted artists from around the world who brought these stories to life through their creative vision and extraordinary talents.

I must also thank my wife, Leah, whose love and steadfast support have been the greatest gift that God has given me.

Finally, I want to thank the teachers and theologians who have shared with me their understanding of God's Word, all of my parishioners, and especially the children whom I have had the joy to know and watch grow up, including my own children and grandchildren. Through their eyes I have seen the Bible stories anew, and it is in their future that I see God's dream fulfilled.

—Desmond Tutu